Marquinho Aniceto

New paths for music education

Marquinho Aniceto

New paths for music education

Private musical instrument lessons and self-learning

ScienciaScripts

Imprint

Any brand names and product names mentioned in this book are subject to trademark, brand or patent protection and are trademarks or registered trademarks of their respective holders. The use of brand names, product names, common names, trade names, product descriptions etc. even without a particular marking in this work is in no way to be construed to mean that such names may be regarded as unrestricted in respect of trademark and brand protection legislation and could thus be used by anyone.

Cover image: www.ingimage.com

This book is a translation from the original published under ISBN 978-3-330-77245-8.

Publisher:
Sciencia Scripts
is a trademark of
Dodo Books Indian Ocean Ltd. and OmniScriptum S.R.L publishing group

120 High Road, East Finchley, London, N2 9ED, United Kingdom
Str. Armeneasca 28/1, office 1, Chisinau MD-2012, Republic of Moldova, Europe
Printed at: see last page
ISBN: 978-620-8-17386-9

Copyright © Marquinho Aniceto
Copyright © 2024 Dodo Books Indian Ocean Ltd. and OmniScriptum S.R.L publishing group

INDICE

1 PRESENTATION

This publication deals with aspects related to learning the instrument, the current music market, the absence of music teaching in Brazilian schools, private instrument lessons, self-learning, and more specifically addresses professional and amateur musicians.

The book aims to reflect on the processes that characterize musical learning, taking into account the educational and cultural dimensions that underpin the formation of students. It also aims to look at aspects related to music education and its insertion into different classroom contexts at the present time, characterized by easily-appreciated market music, the absence of music lessons in schools and students' anxiety about quickly learning to play a musical instrument.

It is based on research carried out in the field of music education and related areas, as well as collecting data from guitarists in Ouro Preto, Minas Gerais, and consulting articles, magazines and *websites.*

From this brief survey, it became clear that self-learning and private tuition are fundamental potentials for the training of the guitarists investigated, which leads us to reflect on the inclusion of the instrument as a possibility for changing the reality of music teaching in schools. This process of learning music refers to obtaining a way of expressing oneself and is related to the tastes, values and personal experiences of each learner.

Music education in Brazilian schools still has many gaps. One of them refers to the fact that it is included in the school curriculum as compulsory, non-exclusive content, according to Law No.° . 11.769[1] . Music education is implicit in the Art subject, a compulsory component of basic education, but it often survives in a hidden form, in extracurricular activities and community projects, as Alvares (2005) points out. On the other hand, in some cases, mainly in private educational institutes, it has been practiced. However, this is still not enough, since in the majority of these cases, musicalization is not

---

[1] Law No. 11.769, of August 18, 2008, which amends Law No.° . 9.394, of December 20, 1996.

conducted in a systematic way, and its objective is only musical cognitive development, i.e. music as an activity to develop the person's intellect, sounding more like appreciation. The influence of music on children's development is undeniable and has been confirmed by countless studies carried out in different countries and at different times, particularly in the final decades of the 20th century and especially in Brazil at the beginning of the 21st century (FONTERRADA, 2008; SOUZA, 2009; BASTIAN, 2009). However, the number of studies related to the practice of music education in nursery schools is still not significant.

Since the demand for private lessons and self-learning has been on the rise recently, it is up to the community of music educators to mobilize so that the pedagogy, practice and theory of the instrument contribute to overcoming the lack of music teaching in the country's schools. Just as Villa-Lobos defended singing (Canto Orfeonico) as a form of expression, the musical instrument can act as a form of expression and contribute to the implementation of systematic music teaching in schools. It is necessary to create the conditions to transform this reality, because music is a necessary and non-peripheral part of culture, and deserves to occupy a prominent place in the educational system (FONTERRADA, 2008). I believe that music is important in the development of knowledge and human expression.

Music teaching remains outdated and non-exclusive in schools. At the same time, the demand for private lessons and self-learning is growing, which leads us to the following reflection: why not invest in teaching instruments in schools? With this in mind, I interviewed seven of my guitar and guitar students, teenagers and children, who are students at private and public schools in Ouro Preto. The empirical data for this research was collected in February 2015 by administering a questionnaire to my private guitar and acoustic guitar students, consisting of the following questions: 1 - Does the school you study at have a music class? 2 - If so, do you attend? Tell us a bit about the class and your expectations; 3 - Would you like your school to have a class on a specific instrument?; 4 - What motivated you to look for private guitar lessons?; and 5 - What do you expect from private guitar lessons? The students who took part in the survey took the questionnaire home and brought it back to the next class with their answers in writing. Their names have been kept confidential so as not to expose any of them.

2 THE CURRENT MUSIC MARKET CONVERGING ON MARKET MUSIC

Technological advances, the speed of information and the digital age have a direct impact on people's behavior and attitudes. The current, the moment, the phase, fashion, prestige and *status* are all geared towards the market. Today's competitive market demands immediate access to relevant information to help make decisions. The biggest challenge is to transform the benefits of technological developments in the global and Brazilian markets in recent years into opportunities for growth, new forms of remuneration and survival in this market.

That would be a theory more geared towards a more optimized practice! This question sets a very suggestive tone in terms of the evolution of thoughts towards immediacy. A novice guitar student, for example, who has never practiced the instrument, arrives for a lesson and, in the first one, tells you about his musical tastes and the style he wants to learn to play. This student comes up with a question - "How long does it take to learn to play?" - which opens up an interesting discussion. With this question, he shows all his anxiety, desire and expectation of quickly building up his repertoire.

The evolution of students' thinking towards immediacy has a direct impact on the teacher's didactics and pedagogy. All the time, we music educators have to reformulate our teaching proposal and keep up with the student's evolution. Often, the teacher has to get straight to the point with the student. The student has to come with the will, the dedication and the persistence to learn. The teacher needs twice as much of this, as well as the flexibility to redo and adapt the teaching whenever necessary.

In today's market, music and commerce are deeply in tune. Everything needs to be quick and practical. Songs need to have a limited amount of time to be enjoyed: above three and a half minutes, the story and arrangement of the song must already be well defined and told. With this comes a whole *marketing* industry that makes students really crave quick results. Cultural plurality is becoming more and more engaging. In this sense, the concept of culture finds, in Geertz's (1989) understanding, an interpretation that has influenced many scholars, namely that of culture understood as a web of meanings that give meaning to human existence. The territorial extension and diverse colonization contribute to our plurality. Other influences absorbed by the cultural industry, the media and entertainment make up our structure, merging and coexisting with traditions. Cultural diversity places us in a position of comprehensive acceptance within a globalized and constantly changing scenario. New elements and new sounds quickly enter the scene, merging with the market and becoming the new. To exemplify the concepts of cultural plurality, I take as an example the object of study of the Ethnomusicology of Music, that is, "music as culture" (MERRIAN, 1964, p. 20). In today's music market, people find space and the possibility to consume, build identities and move a parallel market created by the new digital media. The so-called digital revolution has enabled a new way of consuming music, without intermediaries, direct, easily and quickly accessible, much cheaper or even free. The new paradigm of the relationship between composer, audience and product has led to severe changes in the functioning of the market structure, consumption and production of musical works. Music is now strongly seen as a "product". The internet and digital technology have transformed the cultural industry market. Now, the consumer acts within a virtual and plural collective space, sometimes enjoying a song that will soon be discarded, in the sense that it will soon be "replaced" by another more successful one. However, this consumer is quite unique and individual when it comes to personal musical choices.

I'm very worried about the future of music education, because practicing music, whether through studying a musical instrument or theoretical study, requires a lot of dedication, persistence, patience and discipline. Obtaining the technique of the instrument requires a lot of investment, through frequent repetitive movements. The technique must be in function of the music, an idea that softens the many repetitive movements, but hardly controls the immediacy carried by exacerbated anxiety. An extreme valorization of technique consequently leads to the emptying of music as an educational practice, which results in a lack of pedagogical intentionality. Technique is important, but as a necessity that arises after a practice that creates conditions of possibility for experimentation, exploration, imagination, creation and musical experience. All this is not done without intentionality. This practice needs to be thought about, reflected on and carried out consciously between teacher and student. It has to be something that makes sense to both of them. Now, whether the student, in the face of the current market, with its immediacy and so many distractions, will be able to spend hours practicing and studying their instrument, that's another question.

Faced with the current music market, thinking about music education through private lessons and self-learning aimed at the development of students is a step forward. As the central focus of educational practice, it is important to consider cultural diversity without an extreme preoccupation with teaching technique in a linear and standardized way. I believe that this approach can contribute to discussions about the teaching of music and musical instruments, in Brazil and around the world, with the current music market, and thus help to build a full music education. Music will make more sense to students if their cultural identity is always respected and valued.

3 THE STUDENTS' REPERTOIRE

Music education, in its various contexts of insertion or non-insertion in public or private schools, community social projects and private lessons, brings us a very important topic: repertoire. Knowing the meaning of the musical repertoire built up by the students before they had contact with formal music teaching at school and in non-formal education contributes to pedagogical support that takes into account the students' listening universe. This contributes to understanding their listening experience and to developing strategies for expanding the repertoire of these listening universes, as it values the contextualization of musical understanding and directly influences their interest in musical performance in order to continue learning the instrument.

Depending on the teacher's pedagogy and didactics, in the context of private lessons and self-learning, the content tends to be flexible when it takes into account the students' musical tastes. Thus, my students show me the songs they want to learn and, at the same time, I present a repertoire that I call stages and which is made up of songs that are easy to perform. In the case of beginners, I gradually add elements that make up the progression, such as advanced beats, eyelashes, songs with more chords, etc. The same process can be done with intermediate and advanced students, always thinking about advancing the stages of the specific content for each of them. I often show what each song can teach us in terms of theoretical and practical information, from the simplest to the most advanced. However, for this type of activity to be able to adequately integrate the contemporary classroom environment, it is necessary to respect the varied listening and tastes of the students. It is therefore recommended that the starting repertoire be in line with their preferences, which will then be in dialogue with the other content and the teacher's repertoire suggestions (FREIRE, 2007). It is hoped that this will allow teacher and student to revalue the different cultures present, while respecting their individual experiences. It is important to maintain pleasure, motivation and enjoyment in this teaching process so that, as a result, the student continues to learn the instrument.

Tourinho (1995, p. 236) reinforces our point of view by stating that, "by encouraging students to study what interests them and gives them pleasure, it is possible to obtain better results". In other words, the use of music that is part of the students' daily lives can serve as an ally for the teacher to get to know their optics in relation to their understanding of how they see music, and how their own perspective as a teacher can be associated so that students are presented with other horizons and possibilities. One of the important points to highlight is the possibility of showing students how the content comes together, so that later, the knowledge acquired is the result of everything that has been studied and practiced together, making it possible to listen more sensitively, as well as developing a perception and approach to musical productions from different contexts.

Appreciation can thus be defined as musical training aimed at developing the ability to listen to music intelligently (APEL, 1983 *apud* VOGEL, 2011, p. 41). It is worth emphasizing that the relationships arising from appreciation must be in line with learning musical content and reflecting on the composition as a whole, including its lyrics (in the case of a song), social context, arrangements, instrumentation, etc. According to Franpa and Swanwick (2002), quoted by Massuia (2012), appreciation is a legitimate way of engaging with music in a way that expands understanding and, in general, is accessible to everyone.

The teacher's reflection must be constant, so that the student is always faced with questions such as what makes them like certain music (context, genre, musical structures, instrumentation, etc.) or what made them look for an instrument lesson and study music. The teacher needs to enter the musical universe of the students' preferences, constantly update themselves and try to understand how they learn, what they already know, what they think about music lessons, what their perspectives are, so that they can formulate teaching activities related to these internalizations. Failing to consider this student experience often creates a dislike of music lessons and the repertoire used, which can subsequently discourage the student. In line with Koellreutter (1997), quoted by Queiroz (2014), his pedagogical perspective based on constant questioning and the relationship between music and life, beyond the musical environment and the classroom, aims to construct meanings and the development of critical and creative thinking.

4 INDIVIDUAL GOALS: SOCIAL REPERTOIRE AND RECITALS

Going beyond the confines of private lessons and self-learning is about reaching a certain goal. The study of the instrument and the search for lessons make it clear that there is an interest beyond just learning to play. This attitude is a form of expression that can consequently promote well-being and socialization.

There are many reasons why people seek out private lessons or follow the path of self-learning. I believe in the benefits of contact with music from the first years of life right through to adulthood. In today's world, it is even more evident that music is a great medium in which the student, the musician himself, with his instrument, wants to express himself in a way that makes him feel fulfilled.

On December 3, 2016, I had the opportunity, together with my private lessons students of various ages, to give our first recital at the Casa da Opera Municipal Theater in Ouro Preto. Accompanying them in every step of their dedication and in the joy of their first performance on a stage for the public was meeting different realities. They were brilliant throughout the whole process of the class and also the preparation! They were thrilled with the performance and put on a show! But what stayed with me as a music educator was seeing the way they expressed themselves. For some, it represented their first recital and the opportunity to stand on a stage, and for all, the clarity of the connection between the whole lesson process and self-learning, of wanting to move towards a goal with the contribution of music education, performance and media technology.

I've already had the opportunity to perform recitals with my students at a private school where I worked as a music teacher. Likewise, when I produced the recital, I was able to follow every step of the preparation and the joy of the first performance for many. I was able to meet people from different backgrounds, and they were also brilliant throughout the preparation and performance process! It was very valuable to see how they expressed themselves.

In these opportunities to prepare for recitals, I tried to show my students the importance of committing themselves to the goal. I tried to act in such a way that they could see the steps needed to get to the stage and the importance of

commitment to bringing the best to the public, in a pleasant and uncompromising way, always taking care to respect their ages and

individualities. In the recital of the students who take private lessons at my residence, they gave their opinion on the design of the posters. It was

wonderful to see everyone's joy at creating their artistic name for the

their involvement in the dress rehearsal, their punctuality, the way they dressed and their dedication to practicing the songs. My students began to have a different way of looking at music. Not only them, but also the audience and family members present at the recital, because at each block of the repertoire, we showed videos with testimonies from myself and the students about the benefits and potential of music education. In the recital at this school, because they were younger, it was also precious to see the students' involvement when they learned that the classes held at the school would end with this presentation. They started to dedicate themselves more to it because they thought their families would be there to see them. A special point I would highlight is the involvement of families who want their children to stand out in the presentation. In the school environment, I began to notice that teachers and staff were also interested in the event, involved in setting up the stage and in all the publicity: that's when I began to realize that, during my lessons, some staff always came by to watch the boys play and sometimes even wanted to play for me or ask me questions. So I invited these employees who play or were interested in playing to take part in the recital. This proves that music has the power to mobilize the whole school.

Most of the time, students who have a public performance to give are interested in playing well, focused and busy with their own learning process. Few times is this student in a position to perceive the process they are going through from a perspective that leads them to understand it in all its particular characteristics. Playing what they like has a great influence on this context. As an example of this importance, I would like to point out that in the events I held with my students, each student chose the music they liked and felt comfortable playing. The exception was the children aged between six and seven, as I influenced them to choose music that was easy to play.

In schools in Brazil, since Art is a compulsory subject in the curriculum, music becomes a complementary activity. Teachers from other areas who know how to play an instrument and have a basic musical knowledge end up doing an activity involving music with the students. With the opportunity I had to work as a music teacher at a private school, I realized the need for a professional in the field. In this way, I have always tried to show, in my classes, in presentations at school calendar festivities, and in my relationships with parents, staff and teachers, the importance of music as a subject and beyond the classroom.

5 SCHOOLS WITHOUT MUSIC LESSONS

The absence of music lessons in schools or even the presence of music as a supplementary activity does not fulfill the desire and dream of many students to play an instrument. In the following quotes, referring to the answers to the third question of the questionnaire I administered, my students highlighted their interest in their schools having music lessons. They also commented on which instruments they would like to learn at school:

"Yes, I'd like my school to have violin lessons."

"Yes, if there was a music class, I'd like it to be guitar or guitar."

"I'd like to have lessons on all the instruments."

"Yes, stringed instruments in general."

It can be seen from these answers that students who have a greater interest in learning an instrument tend to look for a music school or private lessons due to the lack of related lessons at their schools. There is also an interest in self-learning because it is an opportunity to learn how to play an instrument.

Self-learning is a personal task that develops the ability to determine their own learning pace, by accessing the content whenever and as often as they want in order to understand what really interests them. This practice facilitates musical development, above all due to the possibility of flexible schedules and content geared towards their main needs. Another detail is that daily interaction with technological resources has led to a musical evolution that enhances this self-learning. The use of the internet, video lessons and handouts is a resource that, over the years, has been constantly changing and, with it, expanding new possibilities. It is necessary to seek awareness of self-learning in music and to deconstruct it as a quality that makes innate talent and the absence of a master unattractive to students. Students can be seduced by the idea that careful study, guidance from a teacher and effort are not decisive factors in becoming a good music professional. The learner may be led to believe that successful, self-taught musicians have not developed a study or dedication to the craft of music. This understanding can discourage and generate an aversion to study and dedication, because when difficulties arise, the stimulus is lost and knowledge tends to stagnate and the student is unable to evolve. It's about the idea that not having a teacher doesn't rule out learning and that learning only takes place in a differentiated, autonomous and flexible way, in most cases. In the classroom, we need to change the notion that hard work is not necessary in music teaching and that inspiration and talent are enough to become an artist. Music educators are key to this.

I believe that Brazilian music is one of the most important expressions of national culture and one of our most internationally recognized cultural products. The song *Garota de Ipanema*, which has been performed and re-recorded all over the world, is a good illustration of this. So why not ask ourselves about the place of music as a compulsory subject in the Brazilian school curriculum? Music is a sub-area of Art, a compulsory component of Basic Education, according to current legislation, but this simply hasn't ensured that it is compulsory. In fact, music survives in the hidden curriculum of the vast majority of mainstream schools, for example in extracurricular activities, community projects, socio-cultural experiences and other variants only when teachers, with some kind of training in the area or not, are interested in adopting it. Other issues also contribute to the lack of effective inclusion of music in school curricula, such as the lack of financial resources to maintain it, adequate physical space, continuity of musical projects, musical instruments and qualified professionals.

Despite the academic support and knowledge of professional and educational associations, the mobilization of various sectors of society, and the high level of sympathizers and pro-justifications, we are faced with the consequent question: how can we put music back on the curriculum? Based on the growing demand for private lessons and self-learning, I see an important factor here: investment in teaching the instrument in schools. Corroborating this statement, I quote Sekeff (2003, p. 108), who says that "music is a form of behavior that stimulates people to think, playing a considerable role in personality development". The author also emphasizes the need to provide students with possibilities to develop their higher faculties, in a constant interrelationship with the development of their sensitivity, emotion and creativity, so that they can live "the wonderful adventure of existing" (SEKEFF, 2003, p. 115). I would also point out that, when practicing self-learning, the student builds his or her own conclusions from a mixture of information from different sources that relate to his or her tastes, values and personal experiences. In general, the tastes and values of student instrumentalists are focused on musical style/genre due to the special position of famous musical groups or virtuoso artists and the help of the mass media in disseminating this personified musical model.

6 MUSIC WORKSHOP

I have the opportunity to work in a private school that has music teaching on its curriculum. It is offered in the form of musicalization and also instrument teaching in the form of a workshop: a specific instrument class offered separately by me. This class takes place at alternative times and in alternative classrooms, after school. Those who are interested start taking the classes by paying a monthly fee to the school and, generally, the students need to have the instrument, even for practicing at home. What can be seen is that music is beginning to re-emerge both as an important part of the pedagogical program at this private school and as a fundamental aspect of the individual's formation. I would like to highlight the interest of students who see these classes as an opportunity to study a musical instrument and play what they love. There are also those who finish regular school and go looking for a private lesson in order to continue studying the instrument. In this experience, the community is also allowed access, including employees of the school itself, parents who are interested in studying the instrument and former students.

It is hoped that the music workshop will have an influence on the students' development in terms of attention in class, school performance, interpersonal relationships between students and teachers, social relationships and emotional behavior. The students find motivation and satisfaction in the music workshop, something new and enjoyable to experience. This reinforces the idea of the importance of music in the school curriculum as an aid to the integral formation of the student.

Parents come to the music workshop because they want to know how important the study of music is for their children's development. Parents want to know how these classes are going, they want to see results, such as their children's performances at school and outside of school, and to understand how music is influencing their child's development. Based on authors such as Gardner (1994) and Garcia (2002), who analyze the mental and psychological aspects of the influence of music on the school life of children and young people, much is expected regarding the value of music in the formation of the individual. Studies such as Garcia's (2002) report how much the brain is activated when music is learned, which may justify its influence on improving learning in other areas of knowledge.

To complement this argument, I would like to refer to the article in the *magazine Galileu-Ciencia* (GARCIA, 2002) which presents research carried out at the University of Heildelberg in Germany, which shows that musicians have 130% more gray matter in the area of the brain corresponding to hearing (primary auditory cortex). This area also houses verbal memory, which is fundamental for learning mathematics, science and languages. The German neuroscientist Peter Schneider says that no one becomes a musician without putting in many hours of study and that some scientists get ideas for their studies precisely through music (GARCIA, 2002). The information processed in the auditory cortex is also related to language, which is why some researchers believe that music is a kind of by-product of language, helping to express speech. Studies such as that by Pantev, cited by Garcia (2002), from the Rotman Research Institute in Toronto, Canada, show that musical functions are concentrated in both the right hemisphere of the brain (intuitive functions) and the left hemisphere (analytical functions). Music also develops Wernicke's area in the brain (important for speech vocabulary), Broca's area (related to grammatical understanding of sentences), develops the brainstem (which helps to localize sound in the sphere) and the cerebellum (a fundamental area for motor coordination). According to Pantev, musical learning also induces plasticity, i.e. the extension of neurons and their connections in the brain.

As the brain is activated in more than four of its areas when the study of music is in action, we can detect its importance in the development of neurological plasticity, which results in an increase in the speed of reasoning, as well as working with the intuitive and perceptive part (right cerebral hemisphere). The aforementioned studies show the importance of musical learning and its relationship with other areas of knowledge for a better education and all-round development of the student.

I would also cite the study by Gardner (1994) who demonstrated that the processes and mechanisms that serve music and human language are distinct. His research showed that in normal individuals without musical training, when any musical activity is required, the right cerebral hemisphere is activated. In individuals with musical training, there are increasing effects on the use of the left hemisphere and decreasing effects on the use of the right. Specifically, the more musical training an individual has, the more they tend to rely, at least partially, on left hemisphere mechanisms (formal and analytical) when solving a task in which a layperson would use right hemisphere mechanisms (purely figurative processing).

We can see the importance of contact with music for the development of the right and left brain hemispheres, which is another strong argument for its inclusion in schools. With music education, we move away from just understanding musical perception (right hemisphere) to looking at it more analytically, with an awareness of the sound process (left hemisphere), thus integrating both perceptual sensitivity and the use of rationality in musical learning. For Gardner (1994), musical intelligence is one of the seven areas of intelligence[2] . The author observed how musical intelligence develops in children from birth and reported that, after the beginning of the school years, there is often little further musical development (GARDNER, 1994). Langer, quoted by Gardner (1994, p. 83), stated that "hardly anyone who has been closely associated with music can refrain from mentioning its emotional implications: the effects it has on individuals". For Gardner (1994), the unanimity of testimonies to the relationship between music and emotion

---

[2] The types of intelligence have been related through intense research at Harvard University in the fields of Psychology, Biology, Philosophy, Anthropology, Sociology and Neuroscience.

suggests that when scientists unravel the neurological foundations of music, the reasons for its effects, its appeal and its longevity, they will be able to explain how emotional and motivational factors are linked to purely perceptual factors.

Music education through a musical instrument, within a regular school, can be feasible and democratize specific and pleasurable knowledge through basic notions of musical perception, technical learning of the instrument and access to reading musical notation[3] . It is also possible to develop and expand a taste for music of different genres and styles, taking into account the student's socio-cultural context and its particularities. It is essential to take action within the government's education policy to guarantee the place of music education in formal education. One feasible solution would be to make time available during the school day for musical activities for all students. As Gardner (1994) and Suzuki (1983) also argue, a democratic music education is one that is available to everyone, without the assumption of selection. Therefore, other fundamental measures would be: adequate physical space, good musical instruments, a broad daily workload, support from the school's management, teaching staff and parents, as well as performances every semester. The work of specialized teachers should be one of the priorities in teaching music in schools. The specialized teacher should be an indispensable stimulator and helper for the enjoyable and efficient learning of music, as well as for its conscious inclusion in the school environment.

---

[3] "Musical notation are the signs that represent musical writing, such as: staff, clefs, notes etc." (MED, Bohumil. *Teoria da Musica*. 4. ed. Brasilia, DF: Musimed, 1996, p. 12.)

7 PRIVATE MUSICAL INSTRUMENT LESSONS

Private instrument lessons represent a significant proportion of the lessons given in today's musical-educational contexts and should be recognized for their role in the musical, personal and socio-cultural formation of individuals. These lessons are characterized by taking place in spaces such as the teacher's home or the student's home, or in other chosen spaces. Private lessons are a type of "alternative music school", where teachers don't need to be qualified, as their teaching skills are legitimized by their work as musicians. Two of the students interviewed gave the following answers as to why they sought out private lessons (question 4 of the questionnaire):

"To have culture and learn an instrument.

"I took the class because I always wanted to learn how to play the guitar."

In this context, just as the spaces and timetables are flexible, so are the contents (instruments, repertoire and theoretical and practical knowledge) covered, since most of the meetings are based on the student's musical tastes and ambitions. Even so, the teacher needs to act as a motivator, as the student has his or her own interests and desires with the instrument and, often, this can go beyond his or her real capacity at the moment. In such cases, it is the teacher's job to be flexible and look for alternatives so that the student doesn't get discouraged.

Lesson objectives are constructed in the interactive process, which generates an educational process. Thus, classes are made possible by a prior agreement between teacher and students, but this can be broken when interests diverge, regardless of the general educational timetables of formal education, although this does not prevent the teacher from teaching some of the content needed to complement the student's education.

Many private teachers, at the beginning of their studies or even afterwards, when they become professionals, maintain the practice of self-learning which is still part of their daily lives. This demonstrates the first link between self-learning and private lessons, and also justifies that type of situation in which the teacher is faced with a student who is well advanced and who, most of the time, has mastered the practical part of the instrument even more than they have.

These self-learning practices go beyond lessons. After all, rehearsing and playing with friends allows students to test what they learn with their private teacher. What's more, deciding on repertoire, the need to play well and the commitment made among friends makes the student take responsibility for their self-learning processes, their private instrument lessons and their content. In this way, individual goals are generated that must be surpassed by the student in agreement with their teacher, as can be seen in some students' answers to the fifth question of the questionnaire, regarding their goals with private instrument lessons:

"Learning and showing what I know."

"I hope to get a good base to be able to play everything."

"I hope to learn to play the guitar in such a way that I can pursue a career in music."

"Learning new ways of playing the guitar."

"Improving my musical knowledge and technique."

One consequence of this is the reference that the teacher has in the community, neighborhood, city, etc., which increases the demand for lessons and, increasingly, the professionalization of this musician and music educator. Through private lessons and the personal search of each student, it is possible to combine elements of non-formal education with formal ones, and to encourage more general practical and theoretical aspects. Students learn by asking questions, observing, reproducing and comparing their teachers, idols (musical models), friends and family. The music teacher becomes a reference point for his students who want to know how he performs, that he records videos, does work and is in full musical activity.

Students look to private instrument lessons for alternatives to overcome difficulties in self-learning and/or improvement. There is no doubt that private instrument lessons currently form a large network of relationships parallel to the formal school system and, at the same time, are recognized by that system, since many schools suggest that students seek out private instrument lessons. Based on the responses of my interviewees, I understand that students have different times and ways of learning and that it is difficult to take into account all these factors that directly influence learning. I realize that there are many possibilities for further study and discussion of private instrument lessons: teacher training, flexibility of timetables, flexibility of pedagogy and didactics, students' personal interests and goals, etc. I believe that one of the challenges is precisely to organize a classroom that, at the same time, is high quality, democratic, with results, that offers quality teaching and is accessible so that all students can learn to play an instrument.

8 PRIVATE LESSONS AND SELF-LEARNING: PLAYING WHAT YOU LOVE

The growing demand for private instrument lessons and self-learning has become a promising path in view of the flexibility with which the whole process is conducted by the student and the teacher and how much this relationship can improve training.

One of the relevant factors in this search is repertoire. All the media connected to music, instruments and performances acts on some personal awakening that becomes desire. The interesting thing is to recognize that students come to lessons with a well-developed mindset about their musical preferences.

In my experience as a teacher, I've been in situations where I've proposed content and repertoire to students. In the first few lessons, I could see their interest in what was new, but after a while, I noticed a certain discouragement caused by low performance. That's why I tried to make it clear that studying music only happens in the long term. I began to notice, in the attitudes of these students (when they talked about a certain singer, a certain band), comments related to hit songs that made them look for lessons. What struck me most was being able to associate the student's attitude with leaving home to look for a private lesson. Reformulating teaching using information from their repertoire was of great value to their learning. It was very interesting to show them the information contained in the songs they liked, which often surprised them.

The demand for private lessons and self-learning has repertoire as the guiding principle for musical study. One learning from this, especially for those who already play an instrument and invest in self-learning, is to be able to reflect, as I learned from my own teacher: "Is my best when I'm playing? Optimize what's best for me". We have many influences. Playing what you don't like is part of the process of studying the instrument.

The repertoire, understood as the set of musical works combined with personal tastes, enhances the construction of knowledge and guarantees more pleasure and fluidity in the studies. So, with my students, I use an expression I learned from my teacher: let them "press *play", I* encourage the idea of playing and playing and building, enriching and increasing the repertoire they really like. The important thing is to make music come out of them. The concepts don't have to be left for later, but should be exemplified in practice, in playing and playing. This creates the habit of being in constant contact with music and the instrument, in a free and pleasurable attitude, which becomes essential in everyday life!

9 WHAT COULD CHANGE MUSIC TEACHING AT SCHOOL

Have you ever thought of a school where students could choose which instrument they would play, either in compulsory classes or in workshops? Which instrument would be part of their compulsory classes during the semester and, at the end, they would present a song played in public as a conclusion?

In recent years, the demand for private instrument lessons and self-learning has grown enormously in various spheres, media and places. The personal fulfillment of playing an instrument and expressing oneself through it goes beyond any methodology in its formal and non-formal aspects, as if the end product, playing a piece of music, were the culmination of all the development. It's a very meaningful process to watch, because from this music that comes out, the limit becomes the next music, with its greater sophistication.

As a musician and music educator, I have worked with private students and have always practiced self-learning. I understand, value and believe that expression through the instrument in various musical styles and genres can contribute to the teaching of music in schools. If we build a "bridge" so that the teaching of the instrument reaches the classroom, we can glimpse a world of many possibilities, from human formation in its various areas, to the evolution of music education itself.

Music teaching still needs to occupy a place where it is as important as any other area of knowledge. Music is one of the ways of expressing art and is free for everyone to experience. Even though music does not occupy a place as a compulsory subject in many schools, it is still always present, in songs, cell phones, sound systems, games and in the learning used as teaching strategies by teachers.

Having a specialized teacher who guides and shows, through research, the importance of contact with the instrument can be very significant for teaching music in schools. Music will always be welcome in a school as long as it is transformative and committed to the growth of the school and the students.

10 SELF-LEARNING AS CONTINUITY IN TEACHER TRAINING

Studies and research carried out by different authors, such as Araujo (2006), Soares, Schambeck and Figueiredo (2014), among others, have helped us to reflect on various aspects that permeate the training of music teachers, such as its legal and normative dimensions, the knowledge that makes up the teaching profession, the role of reflective practice in the constitution of teaching, the relationship between training and professional practice, self-learning as a way of continuing training, the pedagogical projects of degree courses and the foundations and principles for the development of these courses.

These works have provided us with a basis for understanding and realizing the difficult task of training music teachers. This is a task that presents constant challenges, since we are dealing with young people and adults in training, in a world in constant transformation, characterized by the accelerated production of new knowledge and technologies and by all cultural plurality. The training of music teachers is required every semester, with the preparation and practice of lessons. The content needs to evolve in its methodology and concepts.

The current situation is particularly challenging, as it has required higher education institutions to interact more with other areas of society and to embrace diversity, opening up to a greater number of students and, more than that, to other subjects and their knowledge, practices and cultures. In this context, it is essential to strive for quality. Specifically for music degree courses, the challenge is to contribute to the institutionalization of music teaching in primary education.

When it comes to teacher training today, self-learning is a major factor. Curiosity, research and self-interest have opened up a path to knowledge that encompasses the theme of "doing what you love". When you study what you like, with the continuous contact and practice of this exercise, it is expected that it will become a pleasurable attitude that generates expectation and motivation and, consequently, that this practice will become continuous.

Today, with technological advances, there are many online courses that contribute to training and self-learning. Lots of information, materials and other sources are available for study. There are various self-learning processes. As soon as they graduate, teachers need to continue their studies, interests and individual goals in relation to their expectations of professional training and performance. This shows us the situation of our music degree courses in Brazil and is therefore an invitation for teacher trainers, teachers, music undergraduates and instrument students to reflect on their training projects, their training paths and their professional prospects. There are many challenges facing music degree courses, such as investing in the training of teachers for the multiplicity of spaces, both established and emerging, that characterize the field of music education and, at the same time, there are many challenges to ensure that self-learning is, in fact, a process that changes life formation and professional performance.

11 INSTRUMENT PEDAGOGY

Before taking the initiative to start giving private lessons, the teacher needs to realize whether they enjoy giving lessons and believe that everyone can play an instrument. The most important thing is to help that person play an instrument and feel fulfilled. I attribute these processes to more than professional training, which involves character, commitment, patience, persistence and the flexibility to seek out different ways of teaching. Here I defend the idea that the teacher has to be an agent who facilitates the student's understanding of the instrument, relating theory to practice and having knowledge and mastery of application.

So pedagogy, in other words, the teacher's way of teaching, makes all the difference. The student may not like the teacher's didactics, but the teacher has to adapt his didactics so that each student can assimilate the content and studies. In the following excerpt, in response to question 4 of the questionnaire, one of the students investigated highlighted why he came to me to study the musical instrument:

"[...] I had a lesson with another teacher, but he kept playing notes in the first few places on the guitar, and that was it. I couldn't play any songs on the guitar."

Self-formative practice in music is quite common when learning popular music. The fact is that those copied and learned by popular musicians are already "known" and are based on their own taste. They are often heavily disseminated by mass media systems and are part of learners' enculturation processes, which highlights their importance in the learning process. To make it clearer, "when unconscious listening and copying are taking place, the music involved is well known, and one reason why it is known is because it is often heard, the reason for this is that it is appreciated" (GREEN, 2001, p. 68).

Furthermore, when students are practicing something they enjoy, they are not always able to perceive that they are learning something new through the pleasure present in this attitude. I would like to highlight the fact that learning the instrument is a way of expressing oneself, something much more than learning to play, as suggested by the answers of two of the interviewees when asked what motivated them to look for private lessons (question 4):

"As I've been involved in music since I was little and have always enjoyed singing, guitar lessons will help me realize my dream of becoming a professional singer."

"I wanted to learn to play the songs I liked."

For Perrenoud (2000), the notion of competence means the ability to mobilize cognitive resources to deal with different situations. Here are some of the competencies the author describes: organizing and directing learning situations, managing learning progression, involving students in their learning and their work, working in teams, using new technologies, facing the duties and ethical dilemmas of the profession and managing their own continuing education. Teaching competence in educational practice reveals the need for mastery of disciplinary and curricular knowledge, experience and the teaching process, as significant components of the professional role. Another possibility is the idea of the reflective teacher, who, through reflective action, asks questions about their own practice. Reflexivity can be recognized in the study of knowledge, through the focus on experiential knowledge, since it is through everyday experience that teachers begin to articulate their reflexive attitudes with educational practice. I am referring in particular to the situation of valuing and investing in what is working and changing what is not working.

12 PRIVATE TUITION TEACHER

Every music lesson needs to be directed, but in certain situations it is necessary to break away from this system and look for other alternatives for better development and assimilation of theoretical and practical studies. According to Gadotti (2005), formal education has clear and specific objectives and is mainly represented by schools and universities, within a centralized, hierarchical, bureaucratic system controlled at national level by the Ministry of Education's supervisory bodies. Non-formal education is more diffuse, less hierarchical and less bureaucratic, and its programs do not have to follow a sequential and hierarchical system of progression. They can be of variable duration and have the option of granting certificates (GADOTTI, 2005). Santiago (2006), for his part, explains that while the formal teaching of musical practices tends to emphasize the development of technical skills and the study of repertoire, its informal study, typically undertaken by musicians working in the field of popular music, tends to incorporate creative practices such as improvisation, composition, arrangement and playing by ear. Numerous music educators and research musicians recognize the importance of instrumental study that integrates both learning approaches, with the aim of developing a complete musician who masters various conceptions of the instrument and of music itself.

A person who goes to a private tutor wants the teacher's attention. They want to be tutored because, in some cases, they can't discipline themselves in their studies, progress on their own and be self-monitored. They also want quick results. The student looking for an instrument lesson wants a didactic approach that is accessible and in line with their reality and interests. This is why the influence and role of the teacher is so important. It's important that the teacher knows which didactic approach to adopt for the best assimilation and understanding of the student. In private lessons, teacher and student are in an experimental relationship. The student's success depends on a personal connection between teacher and student. If things aren't going well, it's necessary to rethink the plan and find out why it's not working, and to remain flexible. If things are going well, we recommend being optimistic, appreciating and looking forward to all the benefits that music will bring to life.

In this context, the teacher's training, self-study and reformulation of didactics will make all the difference. Private teachers need to have students to support themselves and it is essential that they are up-to-date, active and seen by society. One of the best ways to find a good private tutor is by recommendation, asking friends, neighbors, asking other students for references. It's also important to take a trial lesson, meet and talk to the teacher. Having a teacher who allows you to meet face-to-face is a huge benefit. Some teachers are also willing to go to students' homes for lessons, although this is less common, because when there are only a few students, there is time to go to their homes, but when the timetable is fuller, it becomes practically impossible. It is important to consider the teacher's teaching experience and credentials. The remuneration for the lesson is usually based on this. Realize that you are hiring a teacher to perform a service and know in advance what their policies are and their perspective on practice, payment and recitals. You also need to know their pedagogy and be able to see if there is anything in it that doesn't fit with the student's needs. It's therefore perfectly acceptable to negotiate with the teacher or find another one, which is why the trial lesson is essential. Some teachers advertise in the newspaper, through online classifieds or via social media. Local music stores often have lists of teachers available in *folders* and presentation cards. It is essential to be aware that well-known teachers often have a waiting list. Therefore, it may be necessary for the student to have lessons with another teacher temporarily.

The private musical instrument teacher and the instrumental musician. Some play at night, in bands or do solo work. Some have a bachelor's degree, a degree in music or a technical degree in music. Teachers with a bachelor's degree and a technical degree in music are trained exclusively in music performance. In these courses, the curriculum does not usually provide for the inclusion of pedagogical content in line with the professional situation of the future instrumentalist-teacher, as exemplified by Nieri (2004), in his study, which analyzed the curricula of bachelor's degree courses in the city of Sao Paulo. Due to the specific training geared towards the training of instrumental musicians, the lack of contact with other areas of knowledge, such as pedagogy or psychology, the absence of subjects focused on teaching the instrument and the lack of specific bibliography on the subject available in Brazil, it is common for musicians to have difficulties in complementing their training and, as a result, their didactics are not developed, their interest in teaching is not aroused and the job market becomes limited.

These difficulties have been detected by many music schools and, above all, by instrumental musicians, who are calling for change and have asked their musical instrument teachers to adopt different pedagogical assumptions from those they experienced as students. Most of the time, these musicians have had teachers who come from other backgrounds and from an even more rigid educational context. Depending on the style of music in vogue, the life of concerts and performances has become a competitive market, and not everyone can make it. However, due to the lack of subsidies, courses, research and information that lead instrumental musicians to reflect on the pedagogical practice of their instrument and the conceptual changes in terms of psycho-pedagogical issues that help them to better understand the teaching-learning process, what needs to be done is to change the trend that continues to be the reproduction of the same teaching model they had as students, whether they are aware of it or not, and always observe the student's feedback on the lessons.

In order to reflect on these issues and contribute to their solution, it is important to understand the presence of pedagogical concepts, their conceptual relationships and their unfolding in strategies present in the teaching programs of some schools, higher education and technical courses, in order to reflect on the need or not for music teachers to have pedagogical training. According to my point of view, at some point the musician-instrumentalist will end up needing pedagogical knowledge because, in their career, they may have to teach. Another question would be to find out how they could acquire pedagogical competence.

As the training of the musician-instrumentalist is geared towards performance, but a large proportion of musicians teach their instrument, it is not uncommon for difficulties to arise in dealing with students and in adapting to the methodology of the courses, especially in the early years. Rigidity, lack of flexibility, systematic thinking, not liking or enjoying teaching, the reality of being a graduate are all factors that weigh heavily on students. Frustration can be a major result of this complication. As students on a bachelor's degree or a technical degree in Music with a major in instrument are not prepared to teach, they tend to repeat the teaching models they came into contact with during their training. This can work in some cases, but it can also lead to mismatches and conflicts between teacher and student that could perhaps be avoided if the instrumentalist teacher were better prepared. Especially in private lessons, most of the time the person looking for this opportunity has defined their interests and aspirations and therefore doesn't want a "boring" lesson.

The musician-instrumentalist needs to have a solid background in repertoire knowledge and performance technique, which is offered by bachelor's and technical courses. For this reason, they are the most appropriate professionals to teach their students. To make up for the mismatch between playing and teaching skills and the lack of pedagogical knowledge due to the absence of pedagogical training on these courses, some music schools have required their instrument teachers to complete their training on degree courses. However, these courses are aimed at teaching music in primary and secondary schools, which represents a very different world from the practice of teaching the instrument. There is also a gap in the music degree course. Music teachers in formal schools work with group classes and are bound by an annual school calendar. The instrument teacher, on the other hand, is in a different situation in specific music schools and private lessons, as he or she teaches individual lessons, technique and musical interpretation on the instrument for a period of time that can last for years. In order for the career of the private instrumentalist teacher, whether or not they have academic and/or technical training, to grow, they need to combine all these elements: be pedagogical, didactic, bachelor, researcher, entrepreneurial, practical, constantly working on self-learning and even looking for private lessons.

Aware of this gap in their training, some musicians complement it with extension courses in the field of education. Others come up with their own ways of teaching and learning the musical instrument, often developing intuitive work that shows positive results without the need for specific theoretical knowledge. However, informal observation shows that most teaching musicians repeat the same model they have received without making any significant changes, because their repertoire of pedagogical actions is limited, which becomes a routine of plans and schedules that are the same every semester or year. The student's development is significant and reveals the teacher's didactics, but we also have to consider those students who take their studies beyond the classroom, through self-learning and dedication. In this respect, Louro (1998, p. 106) explains that the musical instrument teacher "challenges the traditional division between a bachelor's degree and a graduate degree, since their training would require them to seek a balance between pedagogical and musical-instrumental skills".

Even though they question the teaching model, many schools and musicians-teachers who imagine they are developing new pedagogical proposals continue to work on the same basis, because they are unaware of the assumptions they are following and have difficulty explaining their own working philosophy. This defines the repetition of an unconscious model that makes teaching stable, prevents the content from evolving and affects student learning.

The basis of the teaching-learning relationship proposed by Rogers (1978) sees learning as a source of personal growth that helps the individual to become increasingly self-aware. The teacher is a facilitator of learning, whose main focus is the student and not the content. His theory prioritizes the student's individual perception and the personal relationship between the student and the teacher. It also values the teacher's consistency and places great importance on the student's self-assessment process. The private student is the private teacher's best didactic and pedagogical guide.

By applying these principles, it is possible to establish that, in order to adopt teaching that focuses on the student and not on the syllabus, philosophical and conceptual changes are needed on the part of the teacher. For there to be a real and considerable change from one model to the other, teachers need to change their way of thinking about teaching, because it is not enough for schools to change the structure of their courses if the professional who will work directly with the student remains stuck in a different conception. In the same way, private teachers must also make this change in model and thinking. According to Rogers (1978), the most important changes are personal, conceptual, related to the vision of the human being and the role of the teaching-learning process in their psychic development. Music teachers need to constantly self-evaluate and observe their students, to see what has been productive and what has not.

13 FINAL CONSIDERATIONS

Music should be on the same level as traditional subjects in formal schools. In the meantime, the tendency to teach it in non-specialized schools is growing stronger. Suffocated for years by a technical curriculum, music is beginning to re-emerge as an important part of the pedagogical program of good private institutes. Among the reasons for music teaching occupying a greater place in school activities is a demand from society itself for it to become a fundamental aspect of the individual's formation.

I can see from my students' answers that the main motivation for seeking out private guitar lessons is their interest in playing music they like and listen to on their instruments. I would also point out that almost all of them answered that the school where they study doesn't have music lessons (questions 1 and 2).

In recent years, there has also been a growing demand for private lessons and self-learning, as most mainstream schools that offer music lessons don't teach the instrument. It is hoped, therefore, that the debate on music education in schools can provide support for more efficient teaching practices and better teacher qualifications. Machado (2004) proposes that the skills needed for pedagogical-musical practice in primary and secondary schools, in the view of music teachers, can be realized in the development of the following abilities: designing and developing music teaching proposals in the school context; organizing and directing "interesting" music learning situations for students; managing the progression of students' musical learning; managing the resources that the school has available for music teaching; gaining appreciation for music teaching in the school context; relating affectively to students, setting and maintaining limits; and maintaining a continuous process of professional training. Confirming the author's proposal, we teachers have to reformulate our teaching proposal all the time and keep up with the student's evolution. That's why it's important that music teaching makes sense to the teacher and, above all, to the student. Faced with the current market, thinking about music education through private lessons and self-learning is a step forward for learning, personal growth and music education.

The starting repertoire should be in line with their preferences, which will come into dialogue with the other content and also with the teacher's repertoire suggestions. It's important to value the contextualization of the students' musical understanding, to maintain pleasure, motivation and enjoyment in this teaching process so that they continue to learn the instrument and achieve good results in their musical performance.

It should be noted that private instrument lessons and self-learning have become a growing path directly linked to personal goals, with repertoire as the guiding principle for musical study. The repertoire, combined with personal tastes, enhances the construction of the student instrumentalist's knowledge and guarantees more pleasure and fluidity in their studies, even though playing what they don't like is part of the process of studying the instrument. There are countless reasons why people seek out private lessons and follow the path of self-learning. It is necessary to search for awareness of self-learning in music and to deconstruct the image of self-learning as a quality that favors innate talent and the absence of a teacher.

The Music Workshop has contributed to the advancement of Music Education, as music has begun to re-emerge as an important part of the pedagogical program of several private educational institutions, and as a fundamental aspect of the individual's formation. Studies report how much the brain is activated when music is learned, which may justify its influence on improving learning in other areas of knowledge. Thinking about the involvement of music in various human aspects reinforces the view of the student as a being who has reason and emotion, as an individual and social being, who has moments of attention and distraction, who needs seriousness to learn, but also moments of relaxation. Music workshops influence school and emotional development. The value of music education goes beyond the limits of an activity of knowledge and aesthetic experience and *status,* and interacts in the development of other dimensions of the human being, such as interpersonal relationships, an aspect that is little valued in teaching, according to Gardner (1994).

Students look to private instrument lessons for alternatives to overcome learning difficulties and/or seek improvement, which highlights the fact that these lessons should be recognized for their role in the musical, personal and socio-cultural formation of individuals. I believe that one of the challenges of these lessons is to foster a good relationship between teacher, student and instrument.

As a musician and music educator, I believe that the personal fulfillment of playing an instrument and expressing oneself through it goes beyond any methodology. I understand, value and believe in expression through the instrument in various musical styles and genres. Music teaching still needs to occupy a place where it is as important as any other area of knowledge. For this to happen, the presence of music educators is essential if music is to occupy a place in school and in the lives of students.

It is of the utmost importance that the music teacher invests in self-learning that is conscious, intelligent, productive and contributes to their training, as this is an opportunity to boost their professional performance. As well as trying to have an exemplary pedagogy of the instrument, it is important for the teacher to exercise character, commitment, patience, persistence and flexibility in seeking different ways of teaching to facilitate the student's understanding. It is also advisable to develop the ability to mobilize various cognitive resources to deal with different situations and to be a reflective teacher.

A person looking for a private lesson wants the teacher's attention. A student looking for an instrument lesson also wants teaching that is accessible and in line with their reality and interests. The teacher's influence is very important at this time. Student success has a personal connection between teacher and student. When it comes to music teaching, the teacher's pedagogy can help the student find their musical development. In order to adopt student-centered teaching, rather than program-centered teaching, changes in philosophical and conceptual ways are indispensable on the part of the teacher, who needs to constantly reinvent his or her way of thinking about teaching.

REFERENCES

ALMEIDA, Cristiane Maria Galdino de. Non-formal music education and professional performance. *Revista da Abem,* n. 13, p. 49-56, Sep. 2005.

ALVARES, Sergio Luis de Almeida. Curricular music education in regular schools in Brazil: the dichotomy between law and fact. *Revista da ABEM,* Porto Alegre, v. 12, p. 57-64, mar. 2005.

AMATO, Rita de Cassia Fucci. A brief historical retrospective and the challenges of teaching music in Brazilian basic education. *Revista Opus,* v. 12, p. 144-168, 2006.

ARAUJO, Rosane Cardoso. Music teacher training: reflexivity, competence and knowledge. *Revista Musica Hodie,* v. 6, n. 2, p. 141-152, 2006.

ARROYO, Margarete. Music education in contemporary times. II SEMINARIO NACIONAL DE PESQUISA EM MUSICA DA UFG, *Anais...* Uberlandia, 2014.

ARROYO, Margarete. Music in Basic Education: situations and reactions in this post-LDBEN/96 phase. *Revista da ABEM,* Porto Alegre, n. 10, p. 29-34, Mar. 2004.

BASTIAN, Hans Gunther. *Musica na escola:* a contribuição do ensino da musica no aprendizado e no convivio social da criança. 1. ed. Sao Paulo: Paulinas, 2009. 288 p.

BRAZIL. *Law no. 11.769,* of August 18, 2008, which amends Law no.° . 9.394, to make it compulsory to teach music in basic education.

BRITO, Teca Alencar de. *Koellreutter educador.* o humano como objetivo da educapao musical. 1. ed. São Paulo: Peiropolis, 2001. 192 p.

DEL BEN, Luciana. Multiple spaces, multidimensionality, set of knowledge: ideas for thinking about the training of music teachers. *Revista da ABEM*, Porto Alegre, n. 8, p. 29-32, 2003.

FONTERRADA, Marisa Trench de Oliveira. *De tramas e fios:* um ensaio sobre musica e educapao. 2. ed. Sao Paulo: Unesp; Rio de Janeiro: Funarte, 2008. 376 p.

FREIRE, Vanda L. Bellard. Conference: Curricula, music appreciation and Brazilian cultures. *Revista Nupeart,* v. 5, n. 5, p. 1-13, set. 2007.

GADOTTI, Moacir. The question of formal/non-formal education. INSTITUT INTERNATIONAL DES DROITS DE L'ENFANT (IDE). *Droit a 'education:* solution to all problems or problem without solution? Sion, Suisse, 18 au 22 octobre 2005. (11 p.)

GARCIA, Marcos da Rosa. Self-learning processes in guitar and private lessons for teaching the instrument. *Revista da ABEM,* Londrina, v. 9, n. 25, p. 53-62, jan./jun. 2011.

GARCIA, Regina. Tuned brains: auditory gray matter reveals secrets of musical talent. *Galileu-Ciencia,* n. 132, p. 67-71, nov. 2002.

GARDNER, Howard. *Structures of the mind:* the theory of multiple intelligences. Porto Alegre: Artes Medicas Sul, 1994.

GLASER, Scheilla; FONTERRADA, Marisa. Musician-teacher: a complex issue. *Revista Musica Hodie,* v. 7, n. 1, nov. 2007.

GEERTZ, Clifford. *The interpretation of cultures.* Rio de Janeiro: Guanabara/Koogan, 1989. 224 p.

GREEN, Lucy. *How popular musicians learn:* a way ahead for music education. London: Institute of Education, 2001.

JUNQUEIRA, Luiz Carlos; CARNEIRO, Jose. *Histologia basica.* Rio de Janeiro: Ed. Guanabara/Koogan, 1971.

LOURO, Ana Lucia; AROSTEGUI, Jose Luis. University teachers / instrument teachers: their conceptions of education and music. *Em Pauta,* Porto Alegre, v. 14, n. 22, p. 35-64, 2003.

MARCONI, Marina de Andrade, LAKATOS, Eva Maria. *Tecnicas de pesquisa.* 2. ed. Sao Paulo: Editora Atlas, 1990. 231 p.

MARCONI, Marina de Andrade, LAKATOS, Eva Maria. *Metodologia cientffica.* 2. ed. Sao Paulo: Editora Atlas, 1992. 320 p.

MASSUIA, Liliana Franco. *The importance of musical appreciation for the development of active listening in the context of musical diversity.* 2012. 25 p. Course Conclusion Paper (Graduation in Music) - University of Brasilia, Open University of Brazil, Brasilia, 2012.

MED, Bohumil. *Music Theory.* 4. ed. Brasilia, DF: Musimed, 1996. (420 p.)

MERRIAN, Alan. *The Anthropology of Music.* Evanston: Northwestern University Press, 1964. 319 p.

NIERI, Debora. *Pianist-teacher:* reflecting on practice. 2004. Dissertation (Master's in Music) - Art Institute, São Paulo State University, São Paulo, 2004.

PENNA, Maura. *Music(s) and its teaching.* 2. ed. Porto Alegre: Sulina, 2010. 230 p.

PENNA, Maura. Music teachers in public primary and secondary schools: a significant absence. *Revista da Abem,* Porto Alegre, n. 7, p. 7-19, Sep. 2002.

PERRENOUD, Philippe. *Ten new skills for teaching.* Porto Alegre: Artmed Editora, 2000. 192 p.

QUEIROZ, Cemy. Considering students' repertoire in music class: a proposal for musical appreciation. Maringa State University (UEM). FORUM DE PRATICAS DE ENSINO DE MUSICA 2014, *Anais...* Maringa, December 3-5, 2014.

ROGERS, Carl R. *Freedom to learn.* 4. ed. Belo Horizonte: Interlivros, 1978. 330 p.

ROGERS, Carl R. *Freedom to learn in our decade.* 2. ed. Porto Alegre: Artes Medicas, 1986. 334 p.

ROGERS, Carl R. *Patient-centered therapy.* Sao Paulo: Martins Fontes, 1974. 525 p.

ROGERS, Carl R. *Tornar-se pessoa.* 2. ed. Lisbon: Moraes Editores. (original work published in 1961).

SANTIAGO, Patricia Furst. The integration of deliberate practice and informal practice in instrumental music learning. *Revista Academica de Musica*, Belo Horizonte, n. 13, p. 52-62, 2006.

SEKEFF, Maria de Lourdes. Music and education. *Revista da Academia Nacional de Musica*, Rio de Janeiro, v. 23, p. 108-117, 2003.

SOARES, Jose; SCHAMBECK, Regina Finck; FIGUEIREDO, Sergio. *The training of music teachers in Brazil.* 1. ed. Belo Horizonte: Fino Trago, 2014. 190 p.

SOUZA, Jusamara. *Learning and teaching music in everyday life. 2.* ed. Porto Alegre: Sulina, 2009. 287 p.

SUZUKI, Shinichi. *Education and love.* Santa Maria: UFSM, 1983. 102 p.

TOURINHO, Cristina. *Motivation and school performance in group guitar lessons:* the influence of the student's repertoire of interest. 1995. 271 p. Dissertation (Master's in Music) - Postgraduate Program in Music, Federal University of Bahia, Salvador, 1995.

TOURINHO, Cristina. Guitar students' musical learning: articulations between practices and possibilities. In: HENTSCHKE, Liane; DEL BEN, Luciana (eds.). *Teaching music:* proposals for thinking and acting in the classroom. Sao Paulo: Moderna, 2003, p. 77-85.

TOURINHO, Irene. Selecting repertoire for music teaching. *Em pauta*, Porto Alegre, v. 5, n. 8, p. 17-28, 1993.

VOGEL, Joane Leticia Araujo. Musical appreciation and the teaching of Music History: an experience report. *O Mosaico: R. Pesq. Artes,* Curitiba, n. 6, p. 41-53, Jul./Dec., 2011.

WILLE, Regiana Blanck. Formal, non-formal or informal music education: a study of adolescents' musical teaching and learning processes. *Revista da Abem,* n. 13, p. 39-48, set. 2005.

ABOUT THE AUTHOR

Brazilian, from Ouro Preto, composer, instrumentalist, teacher and guitarist Marquinho Aniceto comes from a family of musicians and began his career early, at the age of four, accompanying his father and brother and playing at masses. He has a degree in Music from the Federal University of Ouro Preto and a degree from the Bituca Popular Music University in Barbacena, Minas Gerais. He has performed with bands from the city of Ouro Preto and with other artists from the region. He has performed on national television programs such as SBT and TV Cultura in 2015. He has produced, arranged and developed his own works with other musical friends, one of which won 1st place in the popular jury and 2nd place in the general classification at the 1st UFV Music Festival, in Vigosa-MG, in November 2009, with his song *Trilho dos sonhos.* His work of children's songs, *De casa pra escola,* was published at the XX Annual Congress of ABEM (Brazilian Association of Music Educators), in November 2011, in Vitoria-ES. She was the musical producer of the stage-musical show *Crescer: o espetaculo da vida,* with Companhia do Riso de Mariana, in November 2013, at SESI, in Mariana-MG. He gave the workshops *Pedagogia da guitarra e pedagogia do violao and Minha experiencia como musico e educador* musical, promoted by the Music Department of the University of Brasilia, in January 2015 and January 2016, respectively, in Brasilia-DF. He published the poster *How to relate instrument pedagogy to music teaching* and the oral communication *How to relate instrument pedagogy to current music teaching: private lessons and self-learning as new paths* at the X Latin American Regional Conference and the III Pan American Regional Conference on Music Education of ISME - *International Society Music Education*, held in Lima, Peru, in August 2015. He has been taught by great names in Brazilian and international music, such as Mozart Mello, Roger Franco, Andre Scarabelot and Ian Guest. He is a music teacher in the state and private schools in Ouro Preto and a private guitar teacher.

Buy your books fast and straightforward online - at one of world's fastest growing online book stores! Environmentally sound due to Print-on-Demand technologies.

Buy your books online at
www.morebooks.shop

Kaufen Sie Ihre Bücher schnell und unkompliziert online – auf einer der am schnellsten wachsenden Buchhandelsplattformen weltweit! Dank Print-On-Demand umwelt- und ressourcenschonend produzi ert.

Bücher schneller online kaufen
www.morebooks.shop

info@omniscriptum.com
www.omniscriptum.com

Printed by Books on Demand GmbH, Norderstedt / Germany